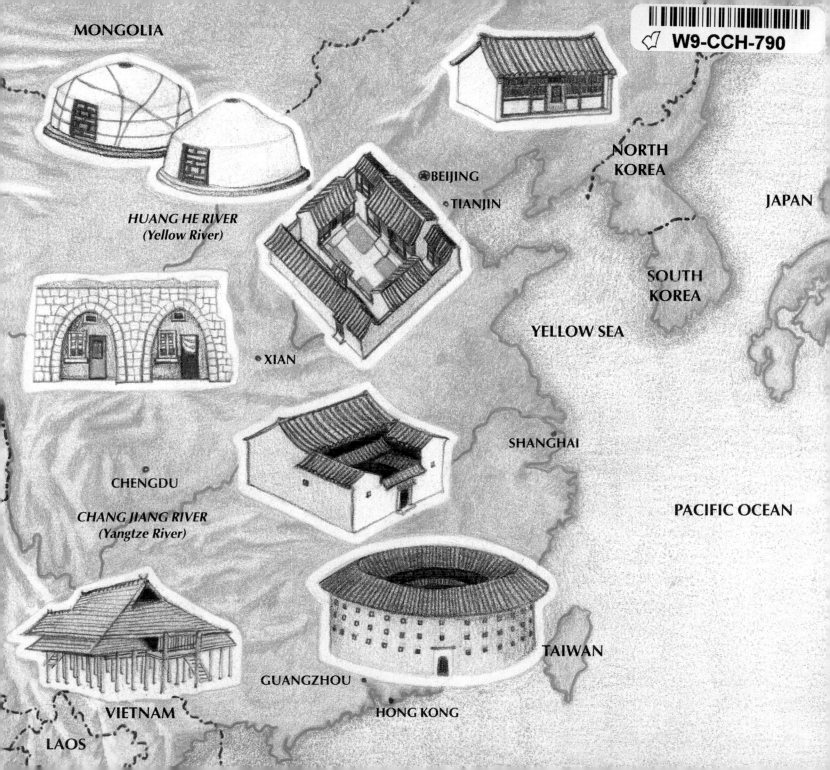

MONGOLIA

NORTH
KOREA

JAPAN

HUANG HE RIVER
(Yellow River)

●BEIJING

●TIANJIN

SOUTH
KOREA

YELLOW SEA

•XIAN

SHANGHAI

PACIFIC OCEAN

CHENGDU

CHANG JIANG RIVER
(Yangtze River)

TAIWAN

VIETNAM

GUANGZHOU•

LAOS

HONG KONG

Houses of China

Tundra Books

Bonnie Shemie

Published in Canada by Tundra Books, Toronto, Ontario M5G 2E9

Published in the United States by Tundra Books of Northern New York, Plattsburgh, N.Y. 12901

Library of Congress Catalog Number: 96-60351

Canadian Cataloguing in Publication Data:

Shemie, Bonnie, 1949-
    Houses of China

Includes bibliographical references.
ISBN 0-88776-369-3

    1. Architecture – China – Juvenile literature. I. Title.

NA7448.S44 1996   j720'.951   C96-900250-5

The publisher has applied funds from its Canada Council block grant for 1996 toward the editing and production of this book.

Design: Sari Ginsberg

Printed in Hong Kong by the South China Printing Co. Ltd.

00 99 98 97 96   5 4 3 2 1

Also by Bonnie Shemie:

Houses of snow, skin and bones. Native dwellings: the Far North
Houses of bark. Native dwellings: Woodland Indians
Houses of hide and earth. Native Dwellings: Plains Indians
Houses of wood. Native Dwellings: the Northwest Coast
Mounds of earth and shell. Native Sites: the Southeast
Houses of adobe. Native Dwellings: the Southwest

Acknowledgments:

My very special thanks to Ronald G. Knapp, professor of geography at the State University of New York, New Paltz, for his invaluable guidance and generous advice; also my gratitude to: Professors Gao Yilan and Shan Deqi of the School of Architecture, Tsinghua University, Beijing; the sculptor, Professor Shi Chaoxiong of Beijing; Professor Zhang Sizan and his student Lin Song, of Xian University of Architecture and Technology, Xian; my new friends, Lui Xiaoli and her husband Zhang Ning of Tsinghua University; and Wu Yan Hong, my wonderful translator, guide and friend at Beijing University; and, lastly, May Cutler of Tundra Books, my prime mover.

Bibliography:

Chang, Chao-kang, and Werner Blaser. *China: Tao in Architecture.* Basel: Birkhauser Verlag, 1987.

Dinsmoor, William. "Mongol Housing with an Emphasis on Architectural Forms of the 'Ger.'" Thesis, Indiana University, 1985.

Faegre, Torvald. *Tents: Architecture of the Nomads.* Garden City, N.Y.: Anchor Books/Doubleday, 1979.

Golany, Gideon S. *Chinese Earth Sheltered Dwellings.* Honolulu: University of Hawaii Press, 1992.

Knapp, Ronald G. *China's Traditional Rural Architecture: A Cultural Geography of the Common House.* Honolulu: University of Hawaii Press, 1986.

———. *China's Vernacular Architecture: House Form and Culture.* Honolulu: University of Hawaii Press, 1989.

———. "Village Landscapes." In *Chinese Landscapes: The Village as Place,* edited by Ronald G. Knapp. Honolulu: University of Hawaii Press, 1992.

Laude, Oliver. "Hekeng Village, Fujian: Unique Habitats." In *Chinese Landscapes: The Village as Place,* edited by Ronald G. Knapp. Honolulu: University of Hawaii Press, 1992.

Lung, David. *China's Traditional Vernacular Architecture.* Hong Kong: Regional Council, Museums Section, 1991.

Schoenauer, Norbert. *History of Housing.* Montreal: McGill University Printing Service, 1992.

Spencer, Joseph. "The Houses of the Chinese." *Geographical Review* 37 (1947): 254–273.

Yoon, Hong-key. "Loess Cave Dwellings in Shanxi Province, China." *GeoJournal* 21 (1/2 1990): 95–102.

Building for good luck

The digging of the cave dwelling began on a day and a place chosen for its good luck. A wind and water interpreter, an expert in the ancient Chinese art of *feng shui*, had consulted a round wooden compass covered with mysterious Chinese characters. This told the most favorable day to begin and the exact site with the best *chi*, or life force, flowing through it, so the family would have good fortune.

For the next three months in the evening hours, the father and uncle worked, using only shovels, a pick and a wooden wheelbarrow. When a large room with a vaulted ceiling had been dug out of the hillside, they finished off the front entrance while the damp interior was allowed to dry out. At last the family could move into their snug new home. Forty million Chinese still live in such carved-out caves in northwestern China.

In trying to shelter their families against difficult climates on difficult land, the Chinese have over the centuries created fascinating dwellings: underground houses, fort-like buildings that can be sealed off from attacks, stone houses built into mountainsides, and, for the powerful, elegant courtyard houses that copy on a smaller scale the great palaces of the emperors of China.

Two main beliefs have influenced Chinese design: *feng shui* and Confucianism. The rules of *feng shui*, developed in the third century BC, govern how, when, and where a dwelling is to be built if the family that will live in it is to have good fortune. The teachings of Confucius (551-479 BC) order how the old and the young relate to each other, the family to outsiders, men to women, and this order is found especially in the courtyard house.

The courtyard house

The elaborate courtyard house was for centuries the exclusive dwelling of China's highest-ranking families. The number of courtyards depended on the owner's place in society, not his wealth. High-ranking families had more courtyards. Buildings were arranged in perfect balance. If a line was drawn down the center, all the buildings on one side would mirror the buildings on the other.

From the street, no one could see behind the gray walls. The entrance, in the southeast corner, faced directly onto a wall. Bad fortune was stopped by the wall, since it was believed that bad luck "ghosts" could not turn corners. The heavy front doors were left open in the daytime, indicating that the family was home, but a high threshold stopped people from casually entering. The outer courtyard was the most public part of the dwelling. Surrounding it were male servants' quarters and storage rooms. A second gate, beautifully carved and called the "hanging flower gate," led into the main courtyard.

There is a feeling of tranquility here. Covered walks allow one to walk around the main courtyard, protected from the rain and sun. In the center are trees and paths. On the right and left are the rooms of the owner's sons, their families, and the female servants. Large extended families living together was believed to bring good

fortune; five generations together in one house was thought to be particularly lucky.

Directly in front is the main building, always a step or two higher than the other buildings, symbolizing its importance. Only high-ranking people or intimate friends of the owner would be invited into this building. The center room, the main hall, is used for ceremonies, such as weddings, funerals and religious celebrations. It is also used as a classroom for the children in the family. On either side are the rooms for the parents.

The kitchen is in the southeast corner of the courtyard, though most of the food preparation is done outside. There are no bathrooms. Basins of water are carried to the rooms for bathing. There is a small privy in a corner of the outer courtyard. Waste is collected daily and taken to the countryside to be used as fertilizer.

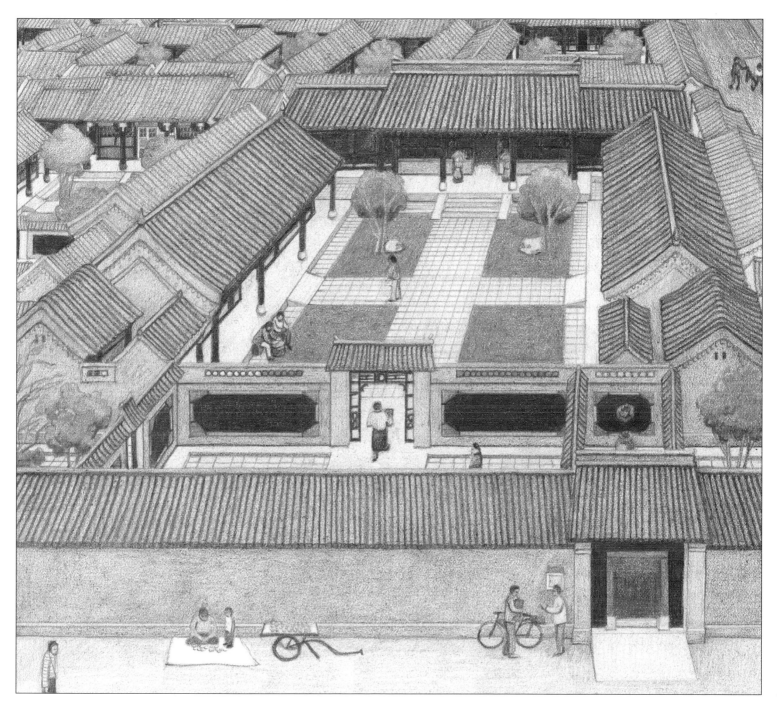

Like an emperor's palace, the courtyard house was orderly, private and serene.

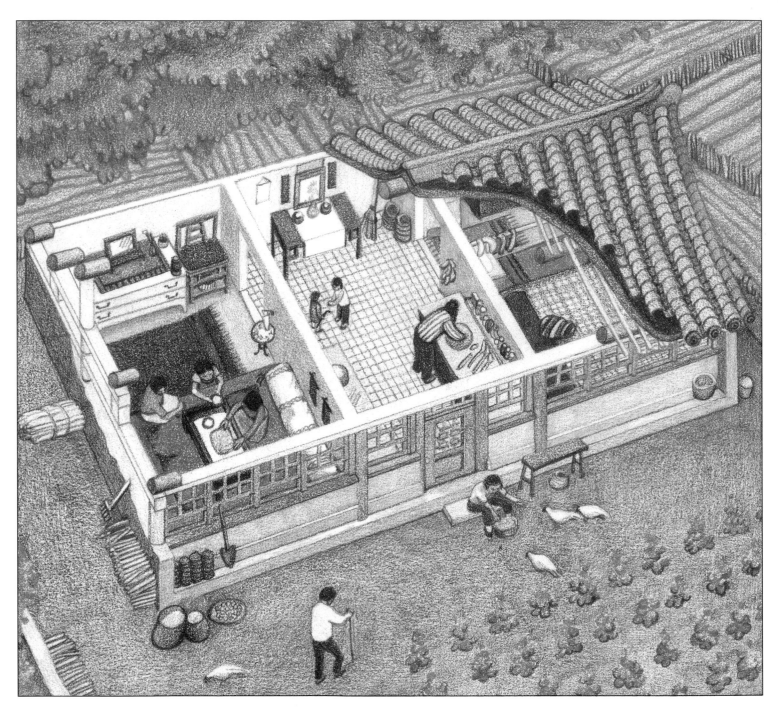

Feng shui and lucky numbers govern the building of even a simple farm house.

The farm house

Although Chinese are now moving to the cities in vast numbers, most still live in simple three-room farm houses and work the land. Wood is scarce because many forests of China disappeared long ago to make way for farms.

According to *feng shui*, it is favorable to have all windows and the single door along the south side, and also to situate the house so that a hill or a row of trees is behind it. There are practical reasons for this as well. The back of the house is protected in winter from the cold winds from the north. The walls are of mud brick, and the pitched roof, made of tiles embedded into clay and straw, extends out over the windows sheltering them from the midday heat. In winter, when the sun is low in the sky, the warm rays penetrate the interior.

A special carpenter's ruler was used when the house was built. It was divided into eight favorable and unfavorable lengths: luck-harm-robbery-rank-justice-separation-illness-wealth. To determine the size of doors and windows and furniture, only favorable sections were used. It was also believed that carpenters and bricklayers could bring bad fortune into the household. If they were not treated with respect, they could hide curses and hexes in the form of drawings or objects made of wood, clay or straw in the structure of the building. The character *xi*, carved into the window design on the front door, means double happiness for newlyweds. The good luck symbol must have worked, if one judges by the presence of so many children. The Chinese are no longer as superstitious as they once were, but they still like to be surrounded by such symbols.

The only door opens into the middle and largest room where a small shrine honors the ancestors. This room is also the kitchen. Farm implements rest along one wall, and a basin holds the morning's laundry ready to be hung out to dry. On the right is the grandparent's bedroom. On the left is the room the children share with their parents. Both bedrooms are heated in winter by a *kang*, a large raised platform made of brick. Pipes running through it carry hot air from the stove in the kitchen. The family sit on a mat on the *kang* to keep warm as they eat. At night, the *kang* becomes a bed.

The fort-like houses of the Hakka

Towering above the countryside in an isolated mountainous region in the southeast of China are dwellings found nowhere else, the fort-like homes of the Hakka. The Hakka originally built these dwellings to defend themselves from outsiders and bandits.

Round or square, three to five stories high, they have a single entrance that can be easily closed off. There are no windows on the first floor and sometimes none on the second floor. A big interior courtyard provides a place for the animals and large quantities of food and fuel. A well is inside for fresh water. It is the perfect place to survive a long siege.

The outer wall of a Hakka house may be several feet thick. Fine yellow silt mixed with lime, brown sugar water, glutinous rice paste, sand and bits of stone is piled into a wooden form to make the base of the wall. It is pounded until it becomes very dense. When it has set, the form is raised up a few feet and the process repeated – rather like our concrete poured walls. Planks supporting the floors are set deep into the earthen wall and joined to the interior wall, which is made of wood. The final dried wall is hard.

A Hakka building may be nearly as large as a football field. Each family lives in rooms that rise from the first floor to the roof, all facing the courtyard. The kitchen on the ground floor holds a stove, fuel, water containers, and cupboards for food and utensils. Next to it another small room has a table, benches, and shelves with dishes. The mother prepares the meals, sews, washes up and does other chores in these rooms or just outside in the courtyard. The family sometimes stands outside the door eating the evening meal while chatting with neighbors.

The second floor is for storage of grain and other food. The third and fourth floors are lighter and airier so they are used as the bedrooms. Unlike western houses, which have their own staircase to reach upper floors, the Hakka building has four staircases that all share.

A highly decorated ancestral hall is the heart of the dwelling and occupies about half the inside space. It houses a shrine commemorating the founding ancestors of the community. The Hakka follow the Confucian practice of showing respect to ancestors in order to gain their protection. The ancestral hall is also used as a study center for the children.

The Hakka are mostly farmers who spend their day in the orchards, vegetable gardens and rice paddies surrounding the village. Women rise early to cook rice and vegetables for breakfast. They may work in the fields with the men, wash clothes in the river, or look after the children. Children play on the paved stone floor of the inner courtyard among the laundry, the baskets of drying rice, the wells and the animal pens.

A Hakka village may have both round and square shaped houses. In round houses, rooms are the same size and there are no dark corners. Some buildings intersect each other so that one can move from house to house without going outside.

Meals are prepared in the kitchen on the ground floor.

The fort-like buildings of the Hakka in southeast China, whether round or square,

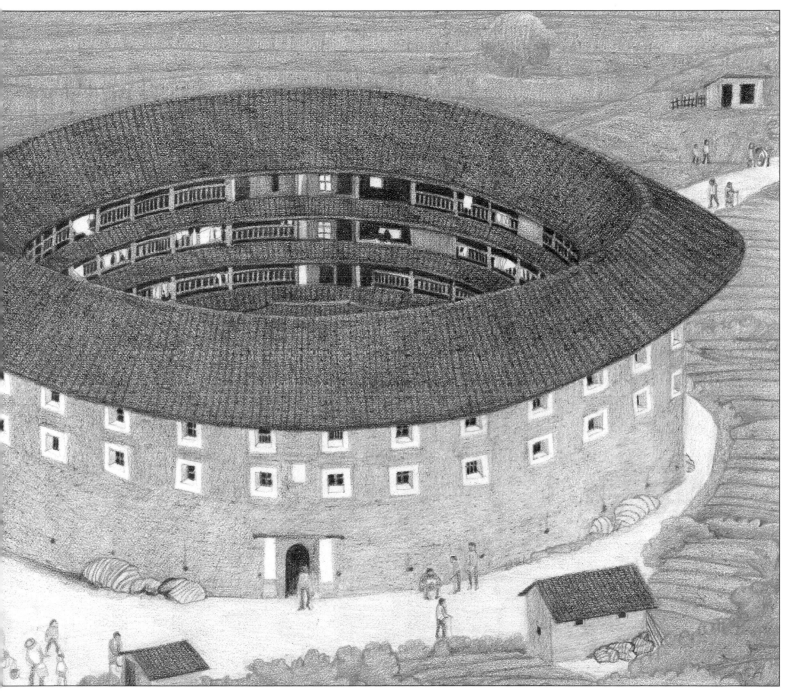

have no windows downstairs and only one entrance easily closed against attacks.

Cutting caves into mountains

Far from the Hakka, in a dry, barren, windblown area of northern China are the cave dwellings. For thousands of years, the Chinese used simple hand tools to carve out these dwellings by either burrowing into the loess cliffsides, or digging rooms underground that open onto an excavated courtyard.

The special earth, a yellow silt called *loess* (pronounced "less") blankets the area at an average depth of thirty-five stories. Loess forms a hard crust when dry and will not collapse during rain storms or excavation. To start the building one must choose a dry location where the loess is pure and free of sand. In cliffside dwellings, this is usually part way up a steep slope that faces south to take advantage of the winter sun. Unfortunately, an ideal site may mean that the family has to walk long distances for water.

As excavation takes place, time is allowed to gradually dry out the chamber. The walls of the room are carved straight up to about the height of a man and curved overhead into an arch. The arch prevents the ceiling from collapsing by distributing the weight of the earth above onto the walls. When fully excavated and dry, the walls are smoothed and surfaced with a thick layer of loess mortar. The floors are usually mud. Wood is scarce and precious, so it is reserved for the door, the window, and a small ventilation hole on the outward face of the cliffside.

The dwelling of a peasant family may consist of only one room. In such a house, along one wall the *kang* is connected to the cooking stove. Along the other wall are a bench, simple farm tools, household goods, and a dresser holding a few clothes.

Cliff dwellings suit the climate. They are warm to live in during the bitterly cold winters and cool in the summer heat waves. They require very little heat in an area where fuel is scarce. Schools, offices and hotels have been constructed the same efficient way.

entrances to cave dwellings

Cave dwellings carved into northern mountains are warm in winter, cool in summer.

Living in an underground house close to the earth is thought to bring good luck.

Carving caves underground

Cave dwellings cut down into the earth on loess plateaus require more digging. Everything is below ground level. The courtyard, open to the sky, is dug first. A stairway is then carved out at the same time so soil can be hauled and distributed on the ground above. When the courtyard is completed and dry, rooms are cut into the side walls as if into a cliff. Bedrooms extend off the south facing side; the kitchen, storage rooms and the pigsty extend off the other sides. If underground water is present, a well is dug in the courtyard. Trees are sometimes planted in the courtyard offering the unusual sight of only their tops showing above ground.

Rooms are built the same as those in cliffside dwellings. They have arched ceilings, a *kang* for a warm bed, and a door, a window and a ventilation opening facing the courtyard. Since the rooms lead onto the open sunken courtyard, they are dark and difficult to ventilate. Some families build additional dwellings on the ground above to use in the summer when humidity is high.

According to *feng shui*, living in the earth brings good luck. Vital energy is said to flow underground and will have a good influence on the families living there. Cave dwellings also conform to other rules of *feng shui*. Sites are dry; the soil is solid, fine in texture, and yellow in color; and important rooms face south. All these conditions are thought to bring harmony and good fortune.

In the cave a single room can look after all family needs.

The yurt can be taken down and put up quickly as herdsmen move from place to place.

The Mongolian "yurt"

Those who live in the sparsely populated, windy, rugged steppes of Inner Mongolia in northern China are nomadic herdsmen. The men spend most of the day on the grassy plains with their large flocks of sheep and goats, and herds of cattle and yaks (large hairy oxen). The women, children and old people remain with the tents. Families must travel from one pasture to another throughout the year and whenever they move, the tents are taken down and put up at the new site.

The tent or *ger* ("yurt" in Russian and English), which can be put up in an hour, is superbly designed to withstand cold and constant wind. Although its dome shape is very stable, it is anchored to the ground in extreme weather. Its walls are made of expandable wooden latticework panels resembling baby gates tied together to form a circle. The door and its frame, made of wood, carved and painted bright colors, faces south. The dome is made of poles connected to a roof wheel in the center and lashed onto the side walls.

The frame is overlaid with two to three layers of thick white wool felt, or cotton-filled quilts kept in place with ropes. Clean white covers are a matter of pride in the community and are renewed frequently if the family can afford it.

The Mongolians are very friendly and like to invite visitors inside to warm up with a cup of black tea and sheep's milk and perhaps to play a game of chess. In the hearth are hot coals. Above it, the roof ring is uncovered so fresh air can circulate. It is good manners not to step on the threshold when entering and to sit in the proper place. Guests sit in a place of honor in the back. The men in the family sit to the left of the door where the men's belongings are stored. Women sit on the right with the women's belongings. The yurt is considered a model of the universe. The roof is the sky, the roof opening is the sun, and the hearth is the earth's sacred center.

putting up the yurt

Tibetan tents of yak hair

Tibet is the home of another group of nomads who live on the highest plateau on earth. Here the valleys are higher than the mountains in most countries, too high for trees. The land is mostly a wasteland of gravel and sand where only a reedy grass will grow. Yet the Tibetan nomads manage to live almost self-sufficiently. Their herds of sheep and yaks provide them with everything they need to survive – transportation, meat, milk, lard, butter to mix with tea or to use as lamp fuel, hair for rope and woven fabric, hide for boots and clothes, and dung for fuel.

Their tents are square, not dome-shaped like the yurt, and black, covered with blankets made from yak hair. The interior of the tent is divided in half by a long narrow stove, built of mud and stones.

Several pots can be heated at once along its length. As winter comes on, the family moves to a sheltered place and piles sod around the tent to help keep out the harsh bitter wind. The sheep and yaks stay in pens and are fed hand-cut hay. For warmth, heavy sheepskin coats are worn over wool garments and rarely taken off. The children used to be sent to school in the capital, Lhasa, and left for months at a time, but now teachers often travel with the families.

Another kind of tent made of cotton and sometimes beautifully decorated with religious symbols is used when many people come together for religious pageants and dramas. Each side of the tent is raised like an awning, so large audiences can watch the events protected from the weather.

the family tent

The Tibetan stone house

In the southern part of the Tibetan plateau, a boy and his little sister play hopscotch on squares scratched into the tamped earth of the flat roof of a stone house. If the children look up, they will see a magnificent view of the valley stretching out for miles below, rich with wild flowers and herbs. On this fertile land farmers grow barley, raise goats, horses, poultry and sheep. Away in the distance are the snowy peaks of the world's highest mountains, the Himalayas.

The four-story house is built into a steep mountain slope. One entrance is into the first floor lower down the slope, the other is into the top floor further up. The stone walls surround wooden floors covered with fine stones and then tamped earth and supported on columns that run through the center of the rooms. The ground floor has pens for the sheep and pigs, a roost for the hens, and a stall for the horses. The family lives on the upper floors.

Family gatherings take place around the hearth in the kitchen on the second level. Big earthenware jars of water, carried from the village well, stand ready for use. In adjacent rooms are stored rolls of butter sewn into skins, barrels of grain, earthenware jars of oil of mustard, and wooden boxes of pastries and rolls. Here, too, meat is hung to dry. On the third floor are the bedrooms, and at the top of the house is the roof

terrace where the children play. Set out to dry along one side of the terrace are herbs for incense, and yak dung and wood for fuel. In the back a specially decorated room is used for family worship. Like most Tibetans, the family devoutly practises a form of Buddhism.

Front doors are draped with decorative banners. The few windows, small to keep out the fierce winds, are richly carved and painted. Though the boy and girl live in a large stone house, their lives are harsh. Even a wealthy family in these remote places has no central heating or running water. On bitterly cold winter evenings, the only heat is provided by coal set in a big brass three-legged firepot and whatever warmth comes up from the body heat of the animals below.

interior of the stone house

In southern Tibet, multi-story houses are built into the steep mountain slopes.

Heat from animals on the ground floor rises to warm those living above.

21

Stilt houses of southern China

Many Chinese who live near the southern border are related to the people of Burma, Laos, Vietnam, and Thailand, and the houses they build show that relationship.

The south is a hot, humid place of terraced fields, lush monsoon jungles, bamboo groves, and rice paddies. Those who are related to the people of Thailand build their houses on stilts to keep away from the damp ground and the insects and poisonous snakes that live there.

A typical home has two rooms and a porch, covered by a massive thatched roof, slanted so the frequent heavy rains can drain quickly. Inside it is dim, simple and bare of furniture. The family sleeps on mats on the floor in one room. In the other, the mother cooks on an open stove set in the center. The porch, sheltered from the tropical sun by the deep overhang of the roof, is like an additional room. Here food is dried, laundry is hung, meals are eaten and the family entertains friends.

Unlike most traditional Chinese dwellings, these houses are built for one family because children are expected to move out after they marry.

Stilts and pitched roofs protect the southern people from monsoon rains.

The HUTONGS of Beijing

The narrow alleys, or *hutongs* (hoo-tongs), that wind and twist through the older sections of Beijing are a wonderful place to see the neighborhood life of China's capital city. The first *hutongs* date back to the time of conqueror Kublai Khan – around 800 years ago. They were lanes that led from dwellings to community wells and horse troughs, or *huts*. As more homes were built, the lanes became lined by the outer walls of courtyards and dwellings. The walls were never high, for it was forbidden to build higher than the imperial palace, or so high that if the emperor should pass, one would be able to look down on him. *Hutongs* became as numerous as "the hair of an ox."

The Chinese have colorful names for their *hutongs*. They can describe who lives there (The Lane of the Bowstring Makers), their shape (Dog Tail Lane), special features (The Alley of the Houses Decorated by Arched Gateways and Carved Bricks), their origin (Mongol Camp), or they may be named after a famous person.

In recent years, the population of Beijing has exploded. In the drive to modernize, many *hutongs* have been destroyed to make way for modern highrise buildings. Behind the old gray walls of the *hutongs* that survive, ten to twenty families crowd into blocks of rooms that look like motel units. Each family has only one or two rooms. Sometimes three generations share a single room. Passageways are a clutter of old stoves, pigsties, piles of coal cakes, bicycles, tiny potted plants, and people: old men playing chess and pedlars selling fruit and vegetables. The *hutongs* are a lively place. Outside toilets and a single tap for water mean everyone learns to share.

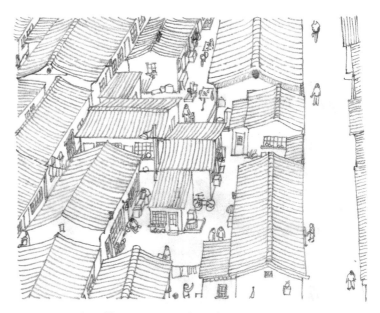

Courtyards off hutongs *with a dozen or more one- or two-room apartments shelter China's city dwellers.*

China, with the oldest continuous civilization on earth, has undergone sweeping changes this century. The traditional courtyard house has almost disappeared; yurts are hooked up to electricity to run televisions and CD players; roads connect remote villages and bring modern technology; peasants are pouring into the cities by the millions. "Five generations under one roof" is no longer desirable, and the *hutongs* are being replaced by skyscrapers. Soon, some of the most unusual dwellings that humans have developed for themselves may be just memories.

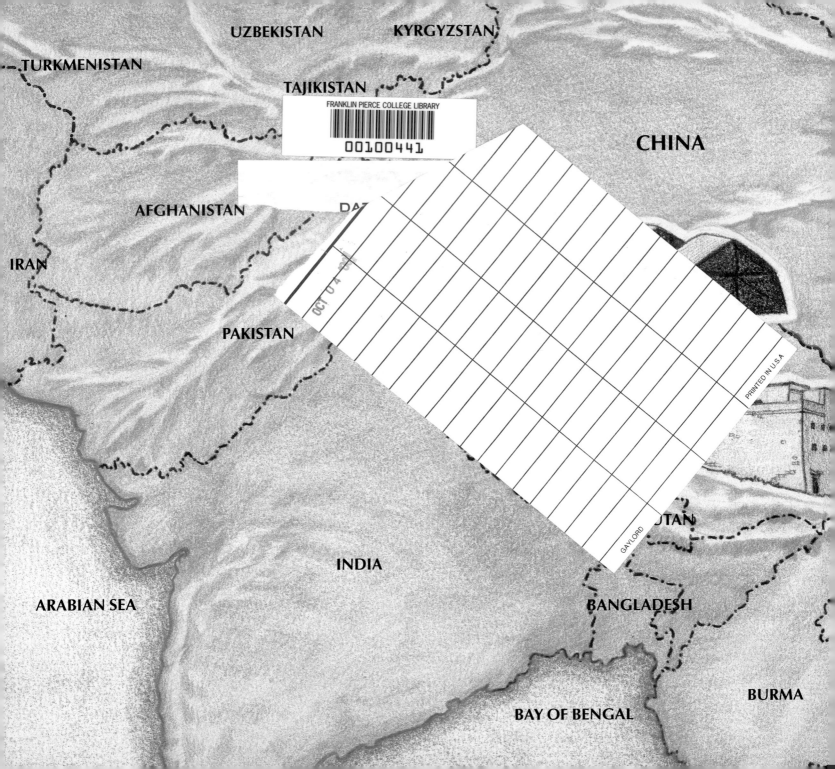

TURKMENISTAN

UZBEKISTAN

KYRGYZSTAN

TAJIKISTAN

CHINA

AFGHANISTAN

IRAN

PAKISTAN

INDIA

ARABIAN SEA

BANGLADESH

BAY OF BENGAL

BURMA